Casablanca

in 3 Days:

The Definitive Tourist Guide Book That Helps You Travel Smart and Save Time

Book Description

Morocco is becoming a more popular destination for tourists, due to its stable government, vibrant culture and its link between North Africa and Europe. Casablanca is taking advantage of this influx of people, and you'll find plenty to do here.

New resorts and hotels are springing up in the historic town, as Casablanca draws travelers who are eager to take in all that this diverse, exciting city has to offer.

Casablanca in 3 Days is the ultimate travel guide for people who don't have a lot of time to spend in one city, yet want to experience as much as they can. It includes:

- The currency type and where to get the best exchange rates
- How to get around in this busy city
- Hotels in three price points, close to various sights

- The main attractions of the city, as well as a few that are off the beaten track
- Restaurants listed by price and specialty, so you can enjoy all the flavors Casablanca has to offer

We have the most up-to-date information and advice on what attractions are worth seeing, and a few hidden discoveries that are off the main tourist tracks. Consider this guide your trusted companion for this adventurous trip.

Begin your journey to Casablanca now!

The People of Casablanca

The city of Casablanca is home to over five million people, and is the busiest city in the region known as Grand Casablanca. 98% of her people live in the urban area. 99+% of the Moroccan population is made up of Berber and Arab Muslims. Early in its history, Casablanca was home to many Europeans, but that number has fallen since Morocco declared its independence in 1956.

If people are a nation's pulse, then the diversity and culture of the people of Casablanca are reflected in every bustling street and byway. Their heritage is long and, although they have begun slowly to embrace modernization, a unique sort of timelessness hangs over them.

Moroccans are quite hospitable. This is a common trait in countries with desert terrain, since traveling was once very difficult. Strangers were given water and food, with the hosts understanding that they might have similar needs someday in the future.

Language

Arabic is Morocco's official language, but about 30% of the population speaks Berber, especially in more rural areas, as well as in the mountains. French is used often in business and commerce, and is taught in schools.

Holidays

January 1	New Year's Day
January 11	Independence Manifesto Day (1944)
May	Labour Day
May	Beginning of Ramadan
June	Aïd al Fitr (End of Ramadan)
July	Throne Day
August	Oued Ed-Dahab Day
August	Revolution Day (1953)
August	HM Mohammed VI's Birthday (Fête de la Jeunesse)
September	Aïd al Adha (Feast of Sacrifice)
September	Aïd al Adha Holiday
September	Fatih Moharrem (Islamic New Year)
November	Green March Day
November	Independence Day
December	Aîd el Maoulid Annabaoui (Prophet's Birthday)
December	Aîd el Maoulid Annabaoui Holiday

Religious Beliefs

Islam is the main religion of Morocco and about 99% of people in the nation are Muslim. This affects the times of day that people are available to assist tourists in Casablanca and other cities. They pray five times a day, the first being at dawn. You will hear the calls to prayer from the mosques' minarets.

Friday is a holy day for Muslims, so some market stalls and shops close at about noon. Muslims normally don't drink alcohol (it is still available for purchase). They do not eat pork (also generally available for tourists) and they don't expose any parts of their bodies.

During Ramadan, the dates of which vary every year, Muslims will not drink, smoke or eat during daytime hours. They are generally tolerant of non-Muslims, though, and tourists, who need to eat. You shouldn't drink or eat in public view, out of respect.

During the month of Ramadan, many places in Casablanca are quieter than at other times of year. Shops may have their alcohol removed from shelves and restaurants are sometimes closed. Things do come to life when evening falls.

Here is a quick preview of what you will learn in this tourist guide:

- Helpful information about Casablanca
- Flying into the city
- Transportation tips in town
- Why Casablanca is such a vibrant tourist spot and what you will find most remarkable about it
- Information on luxury and budget accommodations and what you'll get for your money
- The currency used in Casablanca
- Tourist attractions you should make time to see

- Other attractions for entertainment and culture
- Events that may be running during your stay
- Tips on the best places to eat & drink for all price points, whether you want simple fare, worldwide dishes or Moroccan flavor

Table of Contents

Introduction

Casablanca today is the capital of Morocco in every way other than ceremonially. It's the largest city in the country, and most people who live there are first or second-generation residents.

Often called simply "Casa", this is a new city, and it grew from a small village of fewer than several thousand people, just 150 years ago. Settlers still arrive today, looking for housing, jobs, and a better life than they can achieve in the rural areas of Morocco. Some people actually do make their family fortune here – though most do not – and they display their wealth on the streets and in trendy restaurants and bars. This gives many people the impression that they are in a southern European city.

Casa will never fail to surprise you, as a traveler, by how cosmopolitan and modern it is. Veils are rarely seen, and women and men mix openly, more so than in other areas of Morocco.

Casablanca is still somewhat of a stopping point on the way to Marrakesh and Tangier, and many tourists bypass it. But if you spend even a few days here, the city may grow on you, since it offers nightlife pubs and fine restaurants, and the overall buzz of a city always moving forward.

A Brief History of Casablanca

Casablanca traces her roots back to Anfa, a medieval town. Its location atop a plateau that overlooks the port and coastline, Anfa (which is now an affluent suburb) was the capital of the independent Berber state, after the Islamic Arab invasions, which occurred in the seventh and eighth centuries.

The Merenids took control of the state, then known as Berghouata, in the 13th century. Their dynasty failed during the early years of the 15th century, and local Berbers rose and again took control.

Anfa became a port centered around piracy, and the locals incurred the wrath of the more powerful Portuguese navy. They failed twice to subdue them, but the Portuguese landed finally in 1575. They erected white-washed fortifications and named the settlement Casa Branca, which means "White House". They were subject to many attacks by surrounding tribesmen, but till retained control until 1755.

In that year, the city was severely damaged by an earthquake that also nearly flattened the Portuguese capital of Lisbon. Casa Branca was soon rebuilt by Sultan Sidi Mohammed ben Abdallah, a revered Saadian ruler. He named it Dar al Baida, which is "Casa Branca" in Arabic. The city struggled, however, not regaining its former status, and in 1830, it only had 600 residents.

The Casablanca you see now really only started taking shape in the middle of the 19th century. Europe was by that time flourishing, and nations including Spain, Britain and France eyed the fertile plains of Morocco, as a way to help in feeding and clothing their people.

The region would become a major supplier of wool and wheat, and Europeans visited the city they called Casablanca (a Spanish translation of the Arabic name), to secure agreements for trade.

By the start of the 20th century, France was given permission to build an artificial port that would be larger, to handle the growing demand. Regular supply ship routes soon began to the port city of Marseille. The influence of the Europeans grew rapidly, and even though the whole city prospered, the tolerance wore thin between Moroccans and Europeans.

This tension erupted in violence in 1907, when nine European workmen were killed when they began building a railroad crossing a Muslim cemetery. France sought to increase its Moroccan presence, and they sent in their navy.

After vicious battles between the French and the Berber tribes and locals, the French troops, with a better-equipped force, occupied Casablanca. This was the beginning of colonization, culminating in the 1912 declaration of Morocco as a French protectorate.

The city would become a blueprint for what France wanted to do across the entire country of Morocco. Tangier had already been deemed an International Zone, and the Casablanca harbor was completed, which confirmed its status as the new economic center of the country. Casablanca had become the showpiece of colonial Morocco, with a unique style of architecture that was a combination of Moroccan traditional and French colonial.

French Morocco allied itself with Hitler's Germany in WW II. But U.S. General Dwight Eisenhower landed over 25,000 troops there in 1942. He didn't think the Vichy soldiers would shoot at his men, and he was right. He set his air force base in the city. The classic movie Casablanca, which was based loosely on the events of this time, was shot in Hollywood and released the same year.

Moroccans, meanwhile, were flocking to the new capital city, trying to make money. Some did prosper, but others did not. This resulted in shantytowns or slums, vast in size. By the end of WW II, the population of Casablanca was close to one million people.

The shantytowns were not recognized officially until the end of the reign of Hassan II. He had preferred ignoring the problem. In the early 2000's, many shantytown families were moved by force into blocks of high-rise apartments. The socioeconomic problems were not addressed.

The concentrated areas of poor urban dwellers developed into Morocco's most serious problem, domestically. A coordinated suicide bomber attack in 2003 was attributed to an extremist

Islamist group, whose base was in Sidi Moumen, the largest slum area in Casablanca. This actually directed attention to the plight of the poor. Volunteer organizations moved into the slums, teaching basic reading and IT.

As a casual traveler, you will generally be in the center of the city, and not exposed to Casa's internal discord. The center of town is in the process of a mini-boom, with more restaurants and hotels being built and old hotels being renovated. Casablanca may not have the allure of some regions and cities, but it can be seen as a true reflection of Morocco today.

Neighborhoods

From the markets in the Old Medina to the Art Deco buildings constructed during the French period in Casablanca, the city is full of contrasts.

Casa's central district, where you'll find most attractions, has many of these in a small area, near Mohammed V Boulevard, Mohammed V

Square and United Nations Place. The most popular sights include the Old Medina itself and Casablanca Cathedral.

West of the harbor and the impressively beautiful Hassan II Mosque, Ain Diab is Casa's coastal suburb. It's a trendy area, with many beach resorts, nightclubs and restaurants. In addition to the swimming areas and scenic boardwalk, the highlights include the El-Hank Lighthouse and the shrine and mausoleum of Sidi Aberrahman.

Even farther to the west is Anfa, the city's most affluent residential neighborhood. It's an old neighborhood, and it boasts numerous luxury hotels and grand mansions.

Habous Quarter is southeast of central Casablanca, and is sometimes called "New Medina". It shows off small craft markets (souks) and French colonial buildings. It's also home to the landmark buildings Mohammed V Mosque, the Royal Palace of Casablanca and the Mahakma du Pasha, the court of justice parliamentary building.

What does Casablanca offer its Visitors?

From its home on the Atlantic Ocean to its tall office buildings and main thoroughfares lined with stately palm trees, Casablanca is the economic powerhouse of Morocco. The city is always alive.

The modern buildings blend with charming, older neighborhoods, reflecting the Islamic-Arabic heritage of the city. Wander through the Medina and stroll the downtown area to visit the Hassan II Mosque.

Casablanca is unique – it is perfect for travelers who would rather feel like locals, instead of tourists. You can take the opportunity to experience the present as you view sights from its past. Casa is enormous, and you can set a half-day aside to discover hidden details. You'll find a unique mix of style and grit in Casablanca.

1. Key Information about Casablanca

Money Matters

Morocco's official currency is the Moroccan Dirham. It is abbreviated as Dhs. Each dirham is made up of 100 centimes.

Bank notes can be purchased in these denominations: 20, 25, 50, 100 and 200. Coins can be purchased in these denominations: 1, 2, 5 or 10 Dhs or 5, 10, 20 or 50 centimes.

Main currency can be exchanged at the airport Bureau de Change when you arrive, or at banks or larger hotels. Most of the large hotels can exchange currency at the same rate as you'd pay at the bank, and they don't charge commissions. Do not exchange money on the street, as this is illegal.

When you bring paper currency into the country, like Euros, US dollars or British pounds, they will only be exchanged if they have no ink marks or tears. You cannot cash Northern Irish, Scottish or Gibraltar notes, Singapore dollars or New Zealand or Australian dollars.

Tipping

There is not one set rule about tipping while you're in Morocco. The residents of the country may only leave several dirhams on a dinner bill of 150 dirhams.

If a bellboy carries your bags, 10 dirhams is an appropriate amount, unless you have heavy baggage.

Hotel maids are not paid well at all, so if you have a clean room and fresh towels every day, leave up to 10-15 dirhams per day. Banknotes should be placed inside your pillowcase, so that your own room maid will get it. Otherwise, it may be picked up by the head housekeeper, who might sweep the room when you leave.

Restaurant Tipping

At many high-end restaurants, especially within tourist areas, 10% is added to your bill. If this is the case, you don't need to leave another tip. If your service is poor, don't feel like you have to tip at all. If your service is great, you can leave more than 10%.

2. Transport to and in Casablanca

Getting to Casablanca by Plane

The airport that serves Casablanca is Mohammed V International Airport. It is found in Nouaceur Province, and is managed and operated by the National Airports Office (ONDA). It's the busiest of Morocco's airports, serving almost eight million passengers in 2014.

Getting to Casablanca from the Airport

You can catch a train from Casablanca's airport to the port station and the center of town. They stop just about every hour. Private shuttle companies also wait outside the terminals at the airport, to take arriving tourists and locals into town.

Casablanca Rental Cars

The rental car companies that serve Casablanca include Alamo, Avis, National, Hertz, Budget, Dollar and some local companies. You can find them in Terminal 2 in the arrivals hall. There are signs that point you in the right direction.

Casablanca Cabs

There are two types of taxis that serve Casablanca. Grand taxis are mainly used for transportation from the airport and between cities. They are larger sized cars, often Mercedes, and they are cream or beige colored. They do not use meters. The set fee for travel from the airport to central Casablanca is 250 Dhs or $68 USD.

The Petit taxis, as they are called, will be the ones used in town. They are small and red and have roof racks for luggage. They will not accept more than three riders.

Taxis in Casablanca may be found at taxi stands, or you can hail them in the street as you would in any other major city. If you are traveling by yourself or with one other person, the driver may stop and pick up a third fare, to make more money.

Payment and Tipping for Taxi's

At the airport, taxi drivers may approach you with the offering of a set fare for the ride into town. Do not accept those offers, unless you've been there before, or know that you're not being ripped off.

In the red Petit taxis, check to be sure the meter is on. The drivers are supposed to use the meter at all times, but sometimes they don't turn it on. Taxi rides with set fares are often three or more times higher than rides using the meter.

Minimum taxi fare is set at 7.5 dirhams (Dhs), or $2 USD. If you're using a taxi after 8 PM, there is a 50% surcharge added. By Western standards, Casablanca taxis are usually very cheap. Trips within the center parts of the city should not cost more than about 10 Dhs or $2.72 USD.

To tip your taxi driver, round up your fare to the nearest 5 Dhs – as an example, if the meter says

18 Dhs, adding a tip might bring it to 20 Dhs or $5.45USD.

Public Transport in Casablanca

Casablanca has several choices in public transportation. They include buses, trains and trams.

The buses in Casablanca are useful, but sometimes difficult to figure out. There are various companies, and many routes. The stops can be plotted on Google maps, too, which makes it easier to determine which bus to take.

The different bus companies vary a lot in fare prices. The safest company to use for arrivals and departures is CTM. It is safe and regulated. Avoid smaller bus companies.

The main train station in Casablanca, Casa Port, is larger than it once was, after a recent renovation. The airport train runs from this station to and from the airport.

Casablanca also has a new Tram system, running on a 32 km (20 mile) route system. The original line is being extended and they have begun work on a second line.

Passes & Tickets

Bus costs are 5 Dhs ($1.36 USD) per ride. They are not as comfortable as the trams, but they have the lower price going for them. You may want to just take the tram, unless you're really watching your budget.

Tram rides are 7 Dhs ($1.91 USD) each trip. It's 1 Dhs cheaper or 6 Dhs ($1.63 USD) if you purchase the reloadable tram card. Trams can be caught every 10 minutes or so during the daytime and early in the evening.

3. Accommodations

Casablanca doesn't have the same "feel" or atmosphere as some other cities in Morocco, but it's certainly worth a visit. It's the best representation of the modernization of the country. The money is largely made in Casa, where young people in Morocco travel to seek better jobs. Creative industries and businesses prosper here.

Prices for Luxury Hotels - $140 - $250 USD per night

Four Seasons Hotel Casablanca
- Close to Cathedrale Sacre Coeur, Hassan II Mosque, Casablanca Twin Center, Stade Mohammed V, Place Mohammed V

Hyatt Regency Casablanca
- Close to Hassan II Mosque, Place Mohammed, Cathedrale Sacre Coeur, Complex Cultural Sidi Belyout, United Nations Square

Sofitel Casablanca Tour Blanche

- Close to Hassan II Mosque, Central Market of Casablanca, United Nations Square, Complex Cultural Sidi Belyout, Place Mohammed

Hotel Kenzi Tower

- Place Mohammed, Hassan II Mosque, Parc de la Ligue Arabe, Cathedrale Sacre Coeur, Casablanca Twin Center

Art Palace Suites & Spa - Châteaux & Hôtels Collection

- Close to Hassan II Mosque, Casablanca Twin Center, Place Mohammed V, Parc de la Ligue Arabe, Cathedrale Sacre Coeur

Hotel and Spa le Doge

- Close to Parc de la Ligue Arabe, Hassan II Mosque, United Nations Square, Cathedrale Sacre Coeur, Place Mohammed V

Le Casablanca Hotel

- Close to Hassan II Mosque, Cathedrale Sacre Coeur, Casablanca Twin Center, Stade Mohammed V, Place Mohammed V

Prices for Mid-Range Hotels: $100 - $140 USD per night

Villa Blanca Hotel and Spa

- Close to Boulevard de la Corniche, Place Mohammed V, Hassan II Mosque, Cathedrale Sacre Coeur, Casablanca Twin Center, Stade Mohammed V

La Palace D Anfa

- Close to Maarif, Place Mohammed V, Hassan II Mosque, Cathedrale Sacre Coeur, Stade Mohammed V, Casablanca Twin Center

Ocean Park Appart Hotel

- Close to Hassan II Mosque, Morocco Mall, Place Mohammed V, Stade Mohammed V, Casablanca Twin Center

Sheraton Casablanca Hotel and Towers

- Close to the heart of Casablanca, Place Mohammed V, Hassan II Mosque, United Nations Square, Complex Cultural Sidi Belyout, Central Market of Casablanca

Hotel Gauthier

- Close to Hassan II Mosque, Casablanca Twin Center, Place Mohammed V, Parc de la Ligue Arabe, Cathedrale Sacre Coeur

Novotel Casablanca City Center

- Close to the heart of Casablanca, Place Mohammed V, Hassan II Mosque, Central Market of Casablanca, United Nations Square, Complex Cultural Sidi Belyout

Movenpick Hotel Casablanca

- Close to the heart of Casablanca, Hassan II Mosque, Place Mohammed V, Parc de la Ligue Arabe, Cathedrale Sacre Coeur, Casablanca Twin Center

Prices for Budget Hotels – less than $100 USD per night

Down Town Hotel by Business & Leisure Hôtels
- Close to Hassan II Mosque, Place Mohammed V, Cathedrale Sacre Coeur, Stade Mohammed V, Casablanca Twin Center

Kenzi Sidi Maarouf Hotel
- Close to Hassan II Mosque, Casablanca Technopark, Stade Mohammed V, Place Mohammed V, Hassan II University

Jnane Sherazade
- Close to Habbous Quarter, Hassan II Mosque, Cathedrale Sacre Coeur, Central Market of Casablanca, Parc de la Ligue Arabe, Place Mohammed V

Idou Anfa Hotel
- Close to the heart of Casablanca, Place Mohammed, Hassan II Mosque, Parc de la Ligue Arabe, Cathedrale Sacre Coeur, Casablanca Twin Center

The Seven Hotel & Spa

- Close to the heart of Casablanca, Hassan II Mosque, Place Mohammed V, United Nations Square, Parc de la Ligue Arabe, Central Market of Casablanca

Mogador MARINA

- Close to Hassan II Mosque, Place Mohammed V, United Nations Square, Complex Cultural Sidi Belyout, Central Market of Casablanca

Casablanca Suites & Spa

- Close to Hassan II Mosque, Place Mohammed V, Stade Mohammed V, Hassan II University, Casablanca Technopark

Airbnb's

A modern Tachfine Center Area apartment is available for just $26 per night. It is located right in the heart of town, just a 10-minute walk from Casa Travelers railway station, which connects directly with the Mohammed V Airport. The apartment has a TV area and Wi-Fi, along with a fully equipped kitchen. Fast food restaurants are right up the street if you want to grab a bite to eat.

For just $129 per night, relax in a 2-bedroom, 1 & ½ bath apartment, on the second floor, overlooking a pool. It's just 20 minutes south of the central Casablanca area, located in a secured residential complex in Sidi Rahal. It includes a complete kitchen, a living room and private tennis courts, beach and children's playground.

$173 per night will get you a private suite in a contemporary beachfront villa. It's close to the beach, as well as restaurants, golf courses and horseback riding. There is plenty of outdoor space and great views. It is suitable for single travelers, couples or families with kids.

4.Sightseeing

The commercial center of Morocco, Casablanca, is not as popular with tourists as Rabat and Marrakech, but it's well worth a visit. The traditional Arab culture and French colonial legacy ensure that there are many diverse things to see and do. Near stone medina alleys and art deco buildings, you can find palaces, museums, and one of the largest mosques in the world.

Hassan II Mosque

Nearly every travel guide lists this sight first, and we will, too – because it's the most intriguing attraction in Casablanca, and its largest mosque. The minaret is a dizzying 689 feet high. Atop the minaret is a laser, and the light shines toward Mecca.

Casablanca Twin Center

The Casablanca Twin Center consists of two "skyscrapers", each with 28 floors. The center includes a 5-star hotel and shops, and is in the middle of town, in the Maarif district. The primary architect was a Spaniard, Catalan Ricardo Bofill Levi, and the associate architect was Moroccan Elie Mouyal.

Tahiti Beach Club

Open since 1952, this is a cult of body and sport, and a playful way to enjoy the seaside. You can enjoy the Polynesian-inspired pool, too. The founder was a pioneer in the world of surfing, and he brought the first surfboards to Casablanca from Polynesia in 1950.

Strong currents on the Atlantic coast are great for surfing, which is why this resort is so successful. They have a surf school, if you've never tried surfing but would like to.

The Moorea spa is in the heart of the Tahiti Beach Club, and it is a unique escape from the bustling city. It is a tour for your senses, with massage and Ayurvedic and plantar reflexology massage.

Bouskoura Forest - The Robin Hood Forest

This eucalyptus forest is quite popular, even with locals. It's another chance to get off the flow of people and into someplace that's relaxing. It has good signage and paths, so you won't get lost. You'll also find playgrounds along with tables and benches for relaxing or eating.

Casablanca Market

The mission of the Casablanca Market starts with local artisans who work to create the useful, beautiful products seen there. Each purchase helps local craftspeople and mentors their progress, while preserving their artistic heritage. The craftspeople receive fair market prices for their products, along with the support so vital to continuing to create products.

5. Eat & Drink

The cuisine of Morocco is influenced by the nation's exchanges and interactions with other countries and cultures through centuries past. Moroccan cuisine typically is a mixture of Mediterranean, Arabic, Berber and Andalusian cuisines, with a slight influence from Sub-Saharan and European cuisine.

Fine Dining Restaurants

Le Relais de Paris
approximate price $220 USD for two
Le Relais de Paris is a haven of culinary French delights in Casablanca. Located in the La Corniche area, it offers you a chance to enjoy panoramic sea views while you taste deliciously-prepared French food.

This popular restaurant offers refined style within a comfortable setting, and many enticing flavors. Its mix of modern elegance and tradition entices customers to visit and to return. On their menu, you can choose from meat, fish and even pasta.

Iloli - average price
$110 to $244 USD for two

Diners sometimes call this the best sushi restaurant they've ever been to. The staff are professional and friendly, and the service is excellent. Even though the décor is elegant, you can relax and enjoy the meal. Choose from sushi, fish fillets, miso soup and other tasty dinners, and save room for dessert.

El Cenador - approximately
$158 USD for two

This is the hottest Mediterranean cuisine restaurant in Casablanca. You'll find it on the Corniche, with a great view of the sea. It's elegant and spacious, and its Mediterranean gastronomic cuisine is very popular. You can choose from many fish dishes made in Andalusian style, as well.

Brasserie La Tour - approximate price $163 USD for two

Brasserie La Tour is located under the White Tower's silk-screened glass roof at the Sofitel Casablanca Tour Blanche. You can enjoy French cuisine and wonderful local flavors, prepared with seasonal fresh produce and lots of creativity. From roasted lobster with fresh herb butter and celery cream to risotto with small shellfish and young vegetables and more, you're sure to find a menu item to make your day.

Midrange Restaurants

Rick's Café – approximate price $110 USD for two

This café was made famous by the Hollywood movie Casablanca. It is set in a courtyard style mansion in the Old Medina; it boasts replicas from the film, and a piano bar. Four fireplaces offer private, even intimate, dining, with a fishing port view. The menu specializes in dishes prepared with the freshest vegetables and seafood sourced in Casablanca.

Taverne du Dauphin - approximate price $24 - $90 USD for two

This local favorite eatery is found in the heart of Casablanca, and the prices are reasonable, for what you get. The atmosphere is warm and welcoming, and the staff are very attentive to your needs. They have excellent seafood, oysters and pulpo. You'll be able to tell that everything is fresh.

L'Entrecote cafe de Paris – approximately $34 - $68 USD for two

The motto here is paying attention to the formula of each individual dish. The beef is juice and tender, sliced thin, to your desired level of rare-to-well done. It is served with delicious, delicate beurre maitre d'hotel sauce. They have very reasonable prices for the quality and quantity of food you receive. Save room, if you can, for one of their signature desserts, like les profiterolles or la poire colonel.

Casa Jose – approximately $22 - $44 USD for two

There are many different types of dishes available at Casa Jose. They are all tasty and fresh. They have cold and hot appetizers, and the mains will make it difficult for you to choose just one. Enjoy their fish kebab or shrimp cooked with olive oil and garlic. They also have a great wine selection, and the local white wine is very popular.

Cheap Eats

Le Riad - $8 - $40 USD for two

This restaurant has great reviews, and those people are return diners. You won't be disappointed. The service is prompt and the staff always has a smile for you. They will explain the menu in English to make it easier for you to make a selection. The décor is authentic and so is the food. Try the Chicken Tagine or Caesar Salad. They have plenty of vegetarian and vegan options, too.

Salsa Mexican Grill - approximately $4 - $14 USD for two

This restaurant serves what their fans call "real" tacos and other Mexican dinner items. They are made in a Mexican-American style, not like some local restaurants who serve what they call tacos, but which are actually shawermas (grilled meats served in wraps).

These tacos have sour cream and cheese, just like SoCal tacos. The barbacoa (BBQ) is so tender that it melts in your mouth. You can get "real" sodas here, too, like Mountain Dew and Dr. Pepper.

Restaurant Cafe La SQALA – approximately $8 - $40 USD for two

As soon as you arrive in this eatery, you'll feel welcome. Servers and staff will show you a garden or indoor seat, and will be happy to help you when you're ordering. It's hidden away and locals will recommend it to you. The Moroccan food is just what you'd expect, including their Chicken Tagine with couscous and prunes, and tasty kebabs. They serve different specialties every day.

Americana Café & Grill – approximately $10 - $20 USD for two

A little taste of home – you'll be impressed with their menu. Who could have known you can order a Texas burger and wings in Casablanca, and actually get those authentic foods? They have friendly staff and speedy service, and they even serve pizza. It's a nice place to drop by when you need something you're more accustomed to eating.

6. Culture and Entertainment

The bustling street life of Casablanca is probably a world away from your own city or town. The people and their culture are likely so completely different from what you're accustomed to, and every day can be an adventure. Moroccan culture and art will make your stay more interesting and unique.

Casablanca Cathedral

Casablanca Cathedral, known as the Church of the Sacred Heart of Jesus (in French, as Cathedrale Sacre Coeur), was a Roman Catholic church in Casablanca. Constructed in 1930, the cathedral has not been used for Catholic religious functions since 1956, which was the year Morocco gained independence. It is now a cultural center, and open for visitors.

Musée Abderrahman Slaoui

The Abderrahman Slaoui museum was named after an art collector and businessman who passed away in 2001. It opened in May of 2012. It isn't a large museum, but this is advantageous, since you'll be able to see the exhibits in more detail and without using up a lot of time.

The displayed artwork includes a private collection run by Slaoui's family, ranging from Jaques Majorelle paintings to Asian carvings and glass work. They also have well-curated contemporary art exhibitions.

Place Mohammed V

This is the Casablanca equivalent of Trafalgar Square in London. It features impressive buildings and an illuminated fountain. The most impressive building is the 1920s built courthouse. The clock tower building is the governor's office, known as the Wilaya. The tram now serves this area, so it's very easy to get to from anywhere in the city.

Sinbad Park

Sinbad Park has something for everyone. Amusement park rides will provide fun for the whole family. The zoo contains animals from Wild Africa, Tropical Asia and Madagascar. From gazelles and giraffes to tigers and lions, the habitats are designed to allow the animals to live in much the same way as they would in the wild. Enjoy a quick bite at the food stops or dine in their restaurant.

Casablanca Night-Life

Alcohol is not widely approved of in Morocco, but Casablanca comes the closest of any Moroccan cities to having a busy nightlife. It offers many restaurants, trendy bars and several nightclubs.

The most popular night spots are in the Corniche area. Here, people crowd the beach clubs in the summer months, and congregate in the streets. You may be able to catch some traditional music and dances, too.

Petit Poucet

This bar was once a haunt of famous writer Albert Camus. It's a look back at Casablanca's colonial era. The 1920s décor offers nostalgic ambience. Poucet isn't as easily found as some, but it's a wonderful place for wandering travelers to grab a romantic drink.

La Bodéga

This is a hip tapas bar, found a bit north of the Casablanca central market. They have live music most nights, from Spanish to Arabic beats to reggae and rock music. La Bodega Tuesdays have Brazilian samba lessons. They display sports flags everywhere, and show off the best football matches (for those of you who are Americans, this means soccer, not NFL).

Sky 28

Sky 28 pairs the best views of the city with one of the best wine lists in Casablanca. The tapas is quite delicious and the cocktails are wonderful. They are known for jazz bands that get the nights rolling, and then a DJ spins new jams. The party runs until the wee hours of the morning.

7. Special Events in Casablanca

New Year's Day   January

This is not the Islamic calendar's new year, but January 1st is observed as significant, and Casablanca residents certainly enjoy the day off.

Eid al Adha   February

The actual date of this Islamic feast day varies from year to year. It is also known as the Sacrifice Feast, and is the holier of two Muslim holidays that are celebrated each year, worldwide. It honors Ibrahim's willingness to sacrifice his son on God's command. Allah replaced his son with a sheep to be killed, after Ibrahim passed the test.

Muharram   March

This is also called Islamic New Year. It is celebrated with fervor across Morocco. On the new year for Muslims, alcohol is unavailable in many places.

Eid el Arch   **April**

This is a national holiday celebrating King Mohammed VI's coronation. Casablanca offers a festive atmosphere on this day, with shows, live music and dancing at numerous venues in the city.

Jazzablanca   **April**

Jazzablanca is held in March or April, and is a time for jazz lovers to unite. Acclaimed worldwide groups get together, and new artists are discovered, too. It's a wonderful time for people who love good jazz, and music in general. The gigs are scattered around Casablanca, so many people can experience the jazz.

Al Mawled An Nabawi   **May**

In this festive tine, the people of Casablanca and all over Morocco celebrate the Prophet Mohammed's birth.

Casablanca Festival   July

This is the most significant and popular cultural event held yearly in Casablanca. Venues around the city host art exhibitions, movie screenings, musical events and more.

Révolution du Roi et du People   August

This is the King and People's Revolution Day. It's a public holiday in the city of Casablanca, and it is celebrated by festive activities and parties at various venues, city-wide.

Ramadan   September

This is the most important month on the Islamic calendar. It is observed by abstinence and fasting by the majority of the population in Casablanca.

Eid al Fitr   October

This day marks the end of Ramadan, and it is filled with celebrations. The residents of Casablanca get together with friends and family to enjoy praying, gift giving and feasting.

Fête de l'Indépendance   **November**

This is Morocco's Independence Day and the people of Casablanca celebrate the day heartily, as do people in other parts of Morocco.

Christmas   **December**

The Christians of Casablanca are not many, but they do celebrate Christ's birth, with the same types of traditions you might see in countries that are predominantly Christian.

8.Safety in Casablanca

You will be very unlikely to be in danger in Morocco, but harassment and petty crime do necessitate you to keep your guard up, even more than you do in other countries.

- Women should not walk alone.

Women alone may attract unwanted attention from men. Stay with a friend or your husband, or with a group of people, preferably one that includes men.

- No one should walk alone at night.

Busy and well-lit areas are fine, but don't head down dark streets or alleys. Petty crime is an issue in Casablanca, but you should remain safe if you're in busy areas.

- Don't wear flashy jewelry or carry valuables.

This is true not just for women but for men with expensive watches or rings. If people perceive you as wealthy, they will try harder to rob or scam you.

- Don't leave a purse or laptop bag, etc., sitting out. Keep your purses or bags firmly in hand.

- Dress in a conservative manner.
Morocco is, after all, a Muslim country, and conservative. Don't wear skimpy clothing. You should have your legs, arms and shoulders covered, especially if you're female.

- Negotiate taxi fares before you take off.
Set the price before you and your taxi drive off. Otherwise, the price may be quite inflated when you get to your desired location.

Conclusion

Casablanca today is a big, modern city, but you can still revisit older days in the Old City and Medina. Casa is not as touristy as European cities, but it is as Western and cosmopolitan as you will find in Morocco.

We've given you helpful information for every step of your vacation, from planning and booking a hotel to the best places to eat once you're in town. We showed you some of the premier sights and events, too.

Whatever hotel and restaurants you choose, you're sure to be intrigued by this remarkable city, since it's more surprising than most cities you have visited.

Enjoy your visit to Casablanca!

Printed in Poland
by Amazon Fulfillment
Poland Sp. z o.o., Wrocław

54402505R00034